PEARL

Nuisance

Marcy Schaaf

AF392104

ADULT COLORING BOOK

WELCOME TO "PEARL NECKLACE," A CAPTIVATING ADULT COLORING BOOK THAT INVITES YOU TO EMBARK ON A JOURNEY OF ARTISTIC EXPLORATION AND RELAXATION. UNLEASH YOUR CREATIVITY AS YOU DELVE INTO INTRICATE DESIGNS INSPIRED BY THE TIMELESS ELEGANCE OF PEARLS. EACH PAGE IS A CANVAS AWAITING YOUR PERSONAL TOUCH, OFFERING A THERAPEUTIC ESCAPE FROM THE DEMANDS OF DAILY LIFE.

LIKE A STRING OF PEARLS ADORNING THE NECK, THIS COLORING BOOK WEAVES TOGETHER INTRICATE PATTERNS AND SOOTHING ILLUSTRATIONS, PROVIDING A MINDFUL EXPERIENCE THAT TRANSCENDS THE ORDINARY. WHETHER YOU'RE A SEASONED ARTIST OR SOMEONE SEEKING A MOMENT OF RESPITE, "PEARL NECKLACE" OFFERS A UNIQUE BLEND OF SOPHISTICATION AND SIMPLICITY.

DIVE INTO THE WORLD OF DELICATE SWIRLS, GRACEFUL CURVES, AND ORNATE DETAILS THAT MIRROR THE BEAUTY OF PEARLS. AS YOU IMMERSE YOURSELF IN THE MEDITATIVE ACT OF COLORING, LET YOUR IMAGINATION RUN FREE AND BRING EACH PAGE TO LIFE WITH THE COLORS THAT RESONATE WITH YOU. THE DESIGNS RANGE FROM THE GRACEFULLY UNDERSTATED TO THE BOLDLY INTRICATE, ENSURING THERE'S SOMETHING FOR EVERY MOOD AND ARTISTIC INCLINATION.

EMBRACE THE THERAPEUTIC BENEFITS OF COLORING AND LET "PEARL NECKLACE" BE YOUR ARTISTIC SANCTUARY. ALLOW THE RHYTHMIC STROKES OF YOUR COLORING TOOLS TO TRANSPORT YOU INTO A REALM OF TRANQUILITY AND SELF-EXPRESSION. WHETHER YOU'RE SEEKING A SOLO CREATIVE RETREAT OR A SHARED COLORING EXPERIENCE WITH FRIENDS, THIS COLORING BOOK IS A TIMELESS INVITATION TO UNWIND, RELAX, AND REDISCOVER THE JOY OF COLORING.

SO, PICK UP YOUR FAVORITE COLORING TOOLS, FIND A QUIET CORNER, AND LET THE ENCHANTMENT OF "PEARL NECKLACE" UNFOLD BEFORE YOU. MAY YOUR COLORING JOURNEY BE AS UNIQUE AND BEAUTIFUL AS THE PEARLS THAT INSPIRE IT.

Other adult coloring books available at
www.BooksBySchaaf.com